How to use this book

A sample page

INSTRUCTION
What your child needs to do for the activity.

TITLE
The page title describes the skill your child will learn in these pages.

FUN ILLUSTRATIONS
Specially drawn illustrations which are fun, interesting and drawn at the right pedagogical level for your child.

COLOURFUL BORDERS
The page borders make each page as attractive as possible to stimulate your child.

EXAMPLE
The first one is done for you so you can show your child exactly what to do.

LOTS OF PRACTICE
Two pages where your child can practise and repeat the same skill to master it.

STICKERS
Place a sticker on each page as your child finishes.

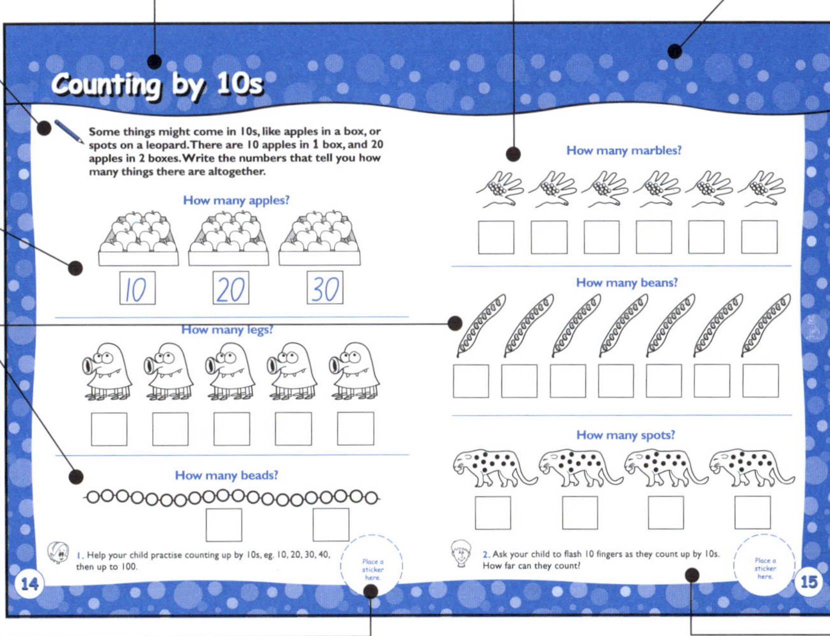

WHO'S HIDING?
In each book, a little creature appears in the border of every double page so your child can have fun trying to find it.

EXTRA ACTIVITIES
Extra activities you might want to do with your child to further reinforce the skill or simply make it more enjoyable.

Step-by-step learning

STEP ONE **Read** out the title of the activity page to your child.

STEP TWO **Explain** the skill and show your child the example already done. **Make sure** they understand what to do. Your child will then have at least two pages to practise that same skill.

STEP THREE **Help** your child put a **sticker** on the bottom of each page as they complete it.

Remember to be patient, encouraging and positive with your child, even when minor mistakes are made!

How to hold a pencil

It is important that you help your child hold their crayon or pencil in the correct way as shown here to ensure your child develops the right technique early on.

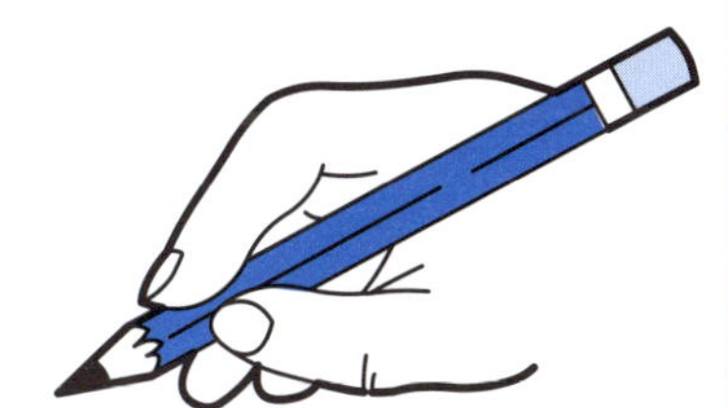

Counting by 2s

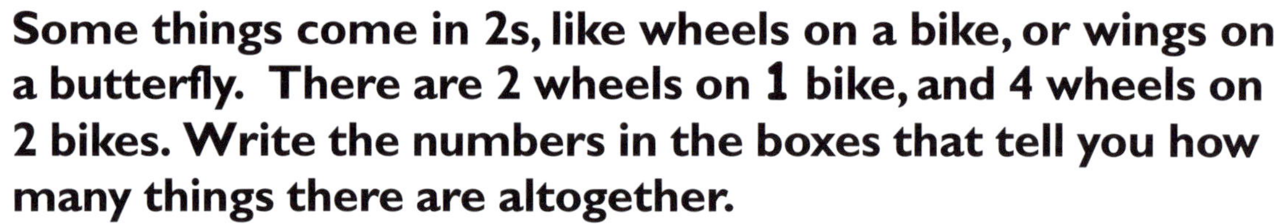

Some things come in 2s, like wheels on a bike, or wings on a butterfly. There are 2 wheels on **1** bike, and 4 wheels on 2 bikes. Write the numbers in the boxes that tell you how many things there are altogether.

How many wheels?

How many beads?

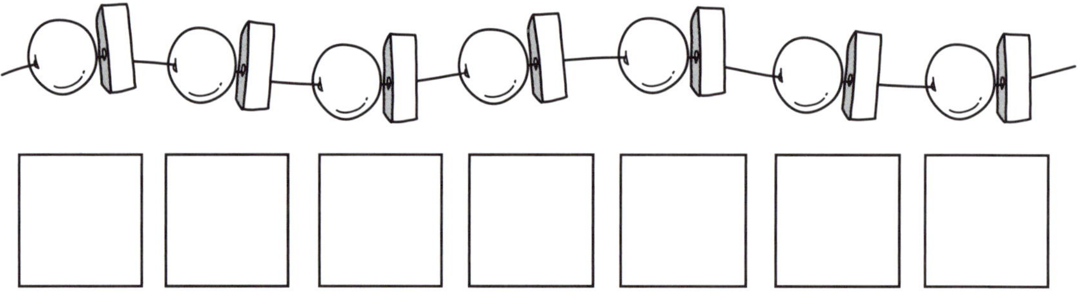

How many wings?

1. What else comes in 2s? Have a look around you for other objects that you can count in 2s.

Place a sticker here.

How many legs?

How many socks?

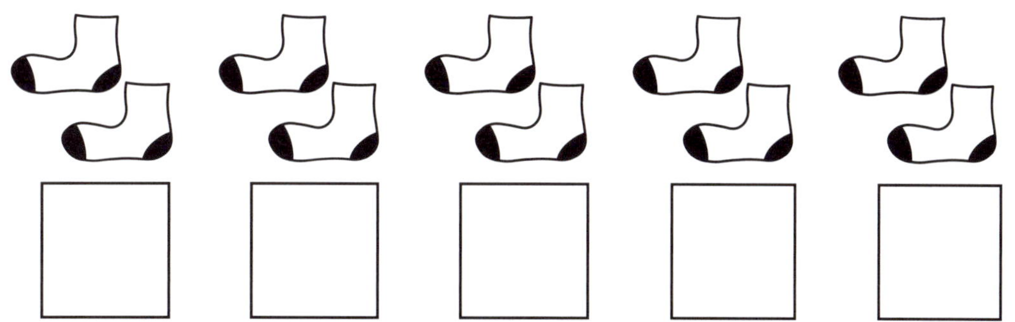

How many triangles?

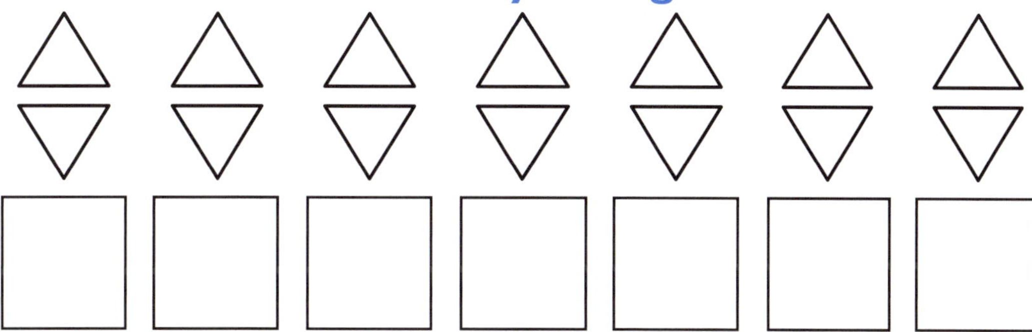

2. Ask your child to count by 2s with their eyes closed.

Place a sticker here.

Drawing groups of 2

Draw the missing pictures in each group. Then count in groups of 2 to find how many there are altogether. Write this number in the circle.

Draw 2 straws in each drink.

Draw 2 sandwiches on each plate.

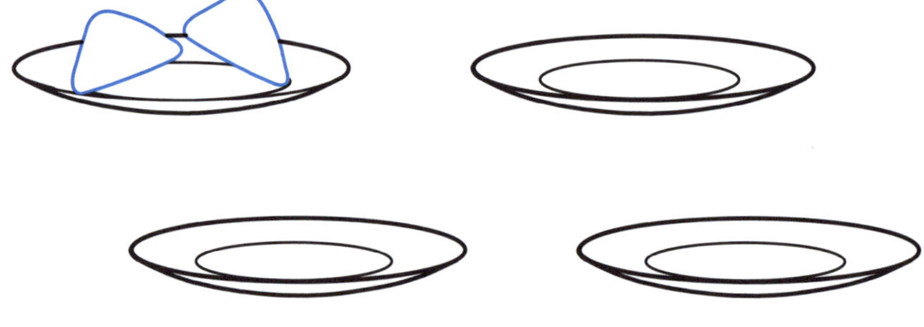

Draw 2 ice-creams on each cone.

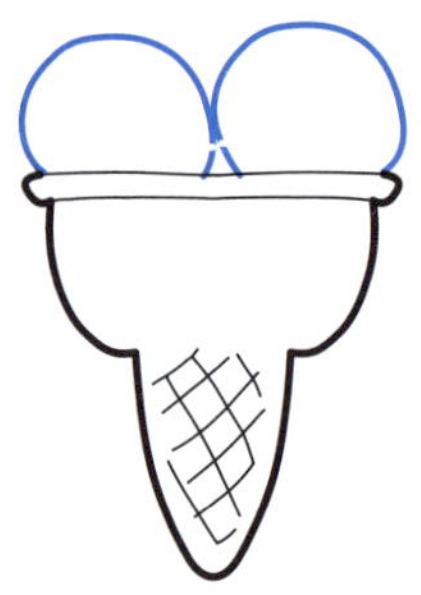

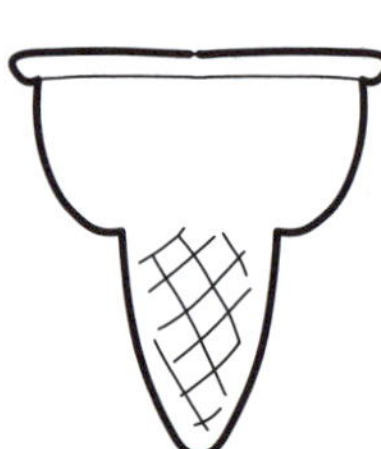

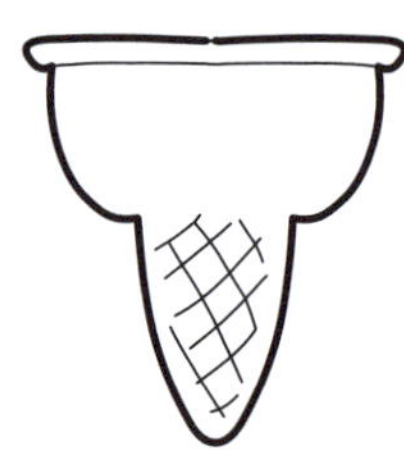

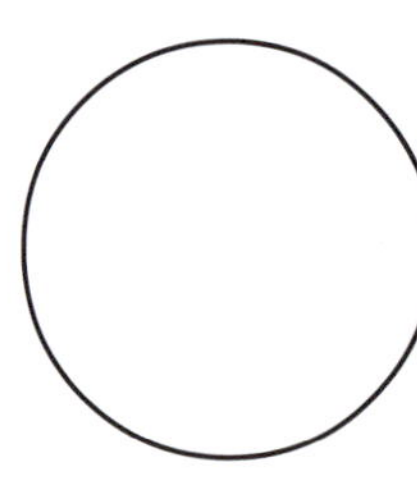

1. Ask your child to count each group of 2 aloud (eg. 2, 4, 6, 8).

Place a sticker here.

Draw 2 olives on each pizza.

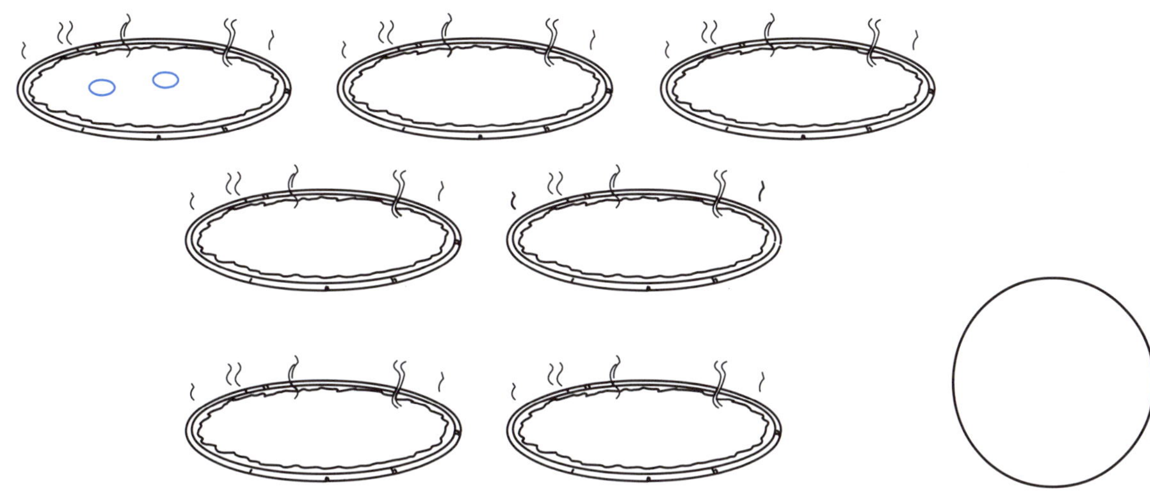

Draw 2 biscuits in each jar.

2. Tip out a pile of toys. Ask your child to put them in groups of 2, then count aloud by 2s to find how many there are altogether.

Place a sticker here.

Drawing more groups of 2

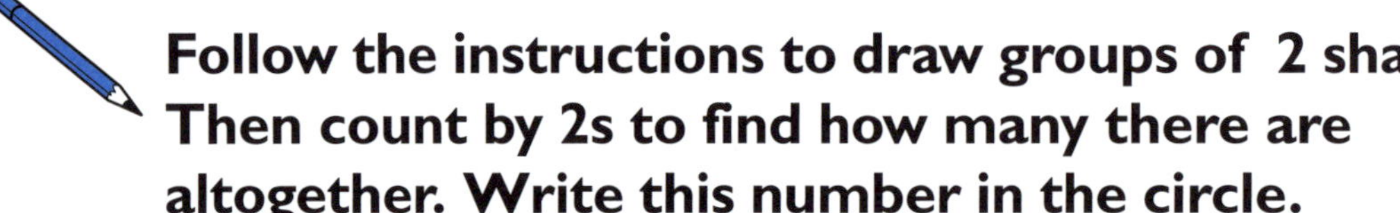

Follow the instructions to draw groups of 2 shapes. Then count by 2s to find how many there are altogether. Write this number in the circle.

Draw 4 groups of 2 triangles.

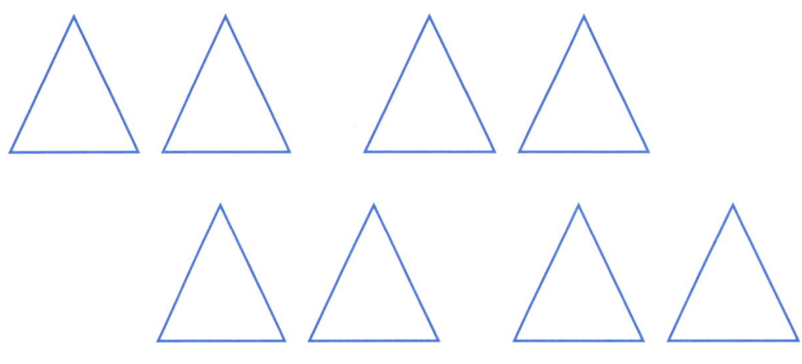

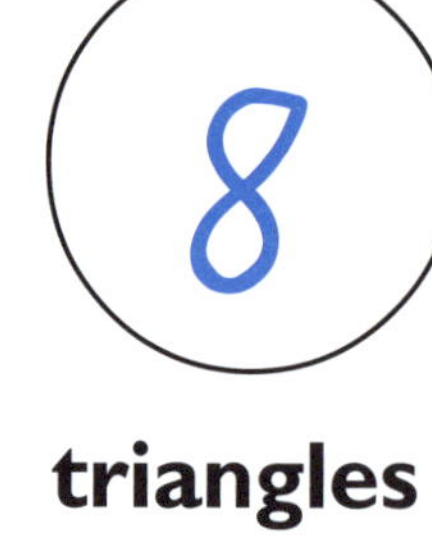

triangles

Draw 2 groups of 2 squares.

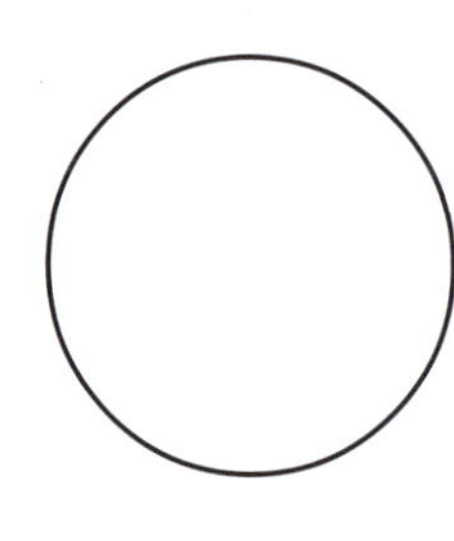

squares

Draw 3 groups of 2 circles.

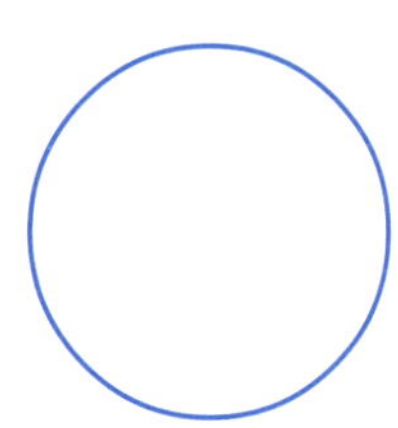

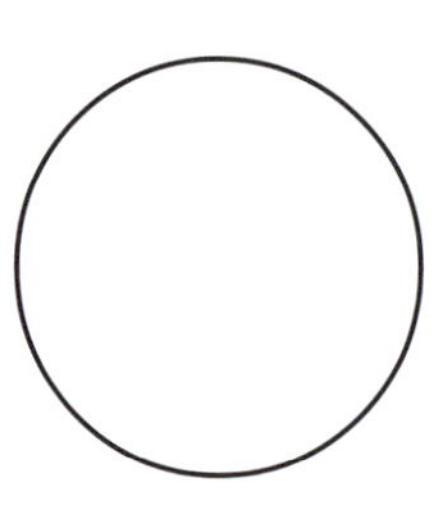

circles

1. Help your child say each 'number story' out loud. For example, '4 groups of 2 triangles makes 8 triangles'.

Place a sticker here.

Draw 8 groups of 2 circles.

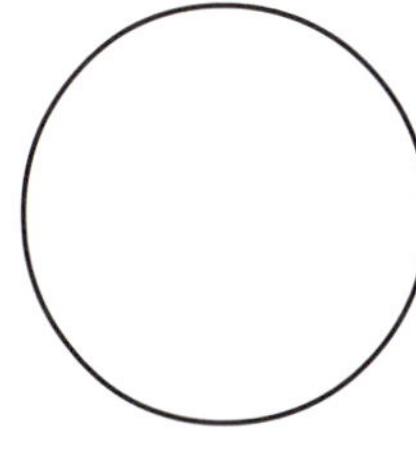

circles

Draw 7 groups of 2 rectangles.

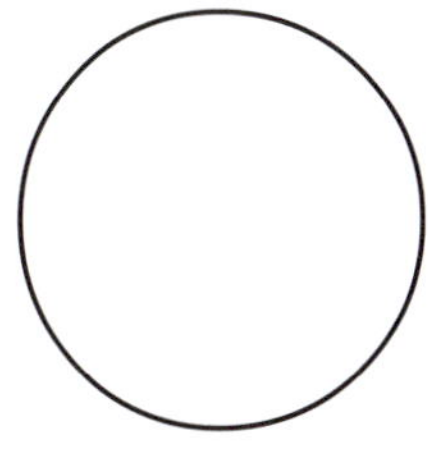

rectangles

2. Cut out magazine pictures and paste them in groups of 2. How many pictures are there altogether?

Place a sticker here.

Finding groups of 2

Count how many animals are in each group. Write this number at the top. Then draw a line around each group of 2 animals. How many groups have you made? Write this number in the square at the bottom.

How many cats? 

groups of 2 cats

How many horses?

 **groups of 2 horses**

1. You can try this activity with real objects, such as small blocks or bottle tops. Ask your child to divide the objects into groups of two, then count them by 2s, eg. 2, 4, 6, 8 and so on.

Place a sticker here.

How many cows?

groups of 2 cows

How many rabbits?

groups of 2 rabbits

2. Ask your child to count each group of 2 aloud (eg. 2, 4, 6, 8 etc).

Place a sticker here.

Making a fair share of 2s

Sharing objects is easy! To share 8 marbles between 4 girls, draw 1 marble in each girl's hand, counting up as you go. Then put another marble in each hand, and keep doing this until you reach 8. How many marbles does each girl have? Write this number in the box. Then do this for each group of pictures.

Share 8 marbles equally between 4 girls.

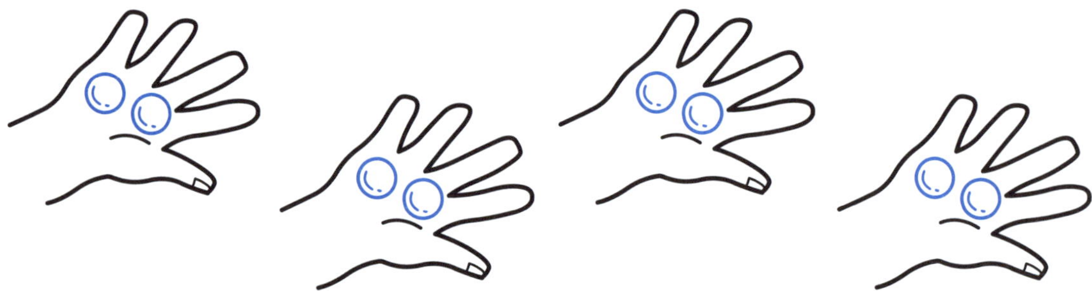

How many marbles each?

Share 6 bones equally between 3 dogs.

How many bones each?

1. Show your child how to add 1 object to each picture, then go back and add another object to each picture, counting up by ones until they reach the total.

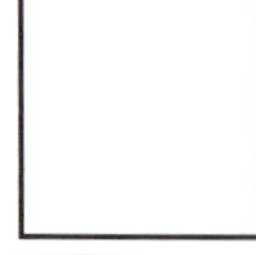

Share 16 fish equally between 8 bowls.

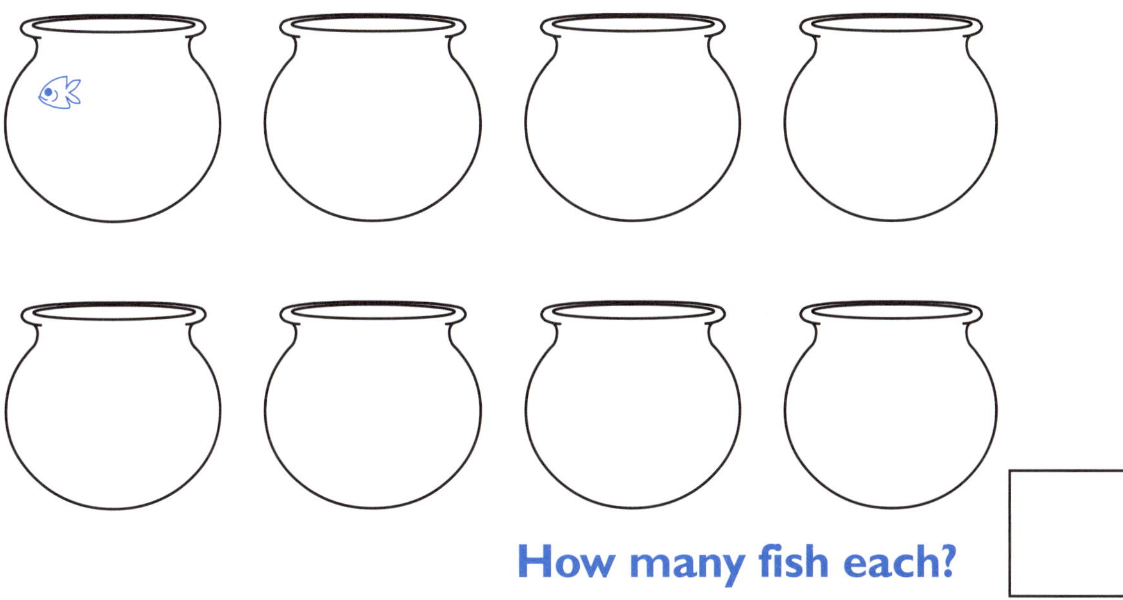

How many fish each? ☐

Share 14 olives equally between 7 pizzas.

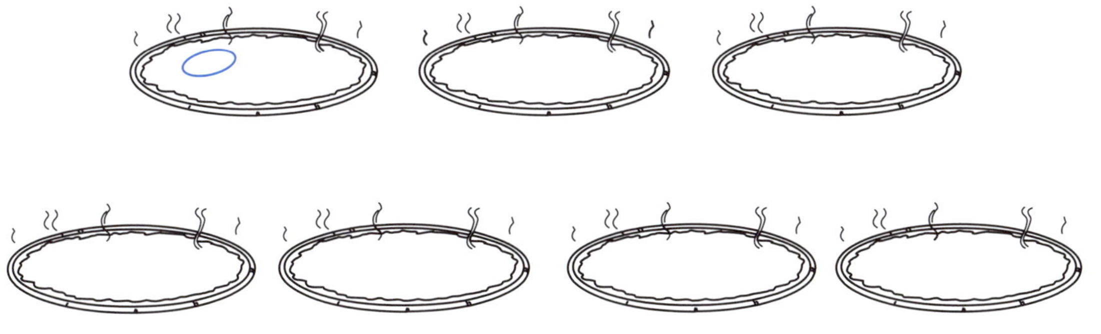

How many olives each? ☐

2. Ask your child to share 12 toys between 6 people.
How many toys each?

Place a sticker here.

Joining the dots by 2s

Here are 2 hidden pictures. What do you think they might be? Start at 0. Count up by 2s and join the numbers in a line to make the pictures. Then join the last number back to 0.

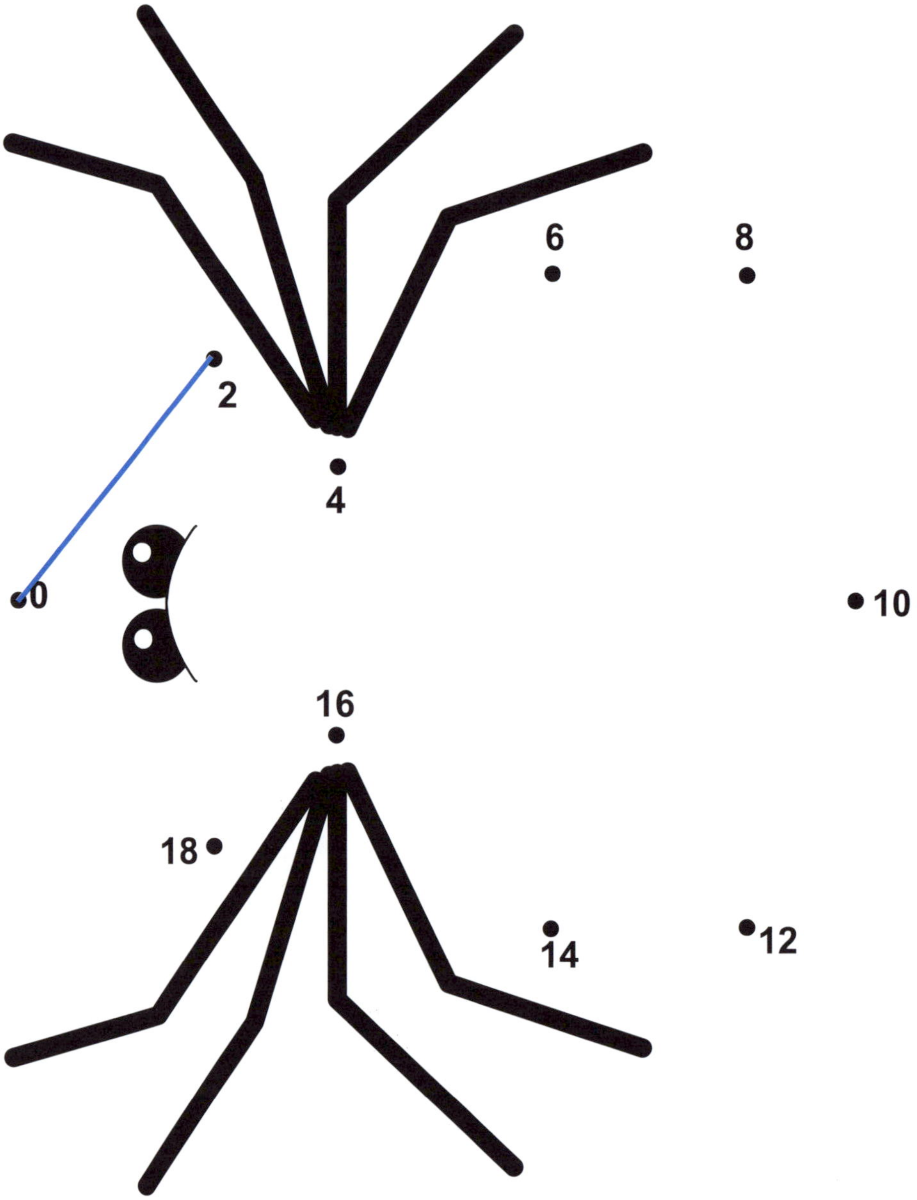

0 2 4 6 8 10 12 14 16 18

1. Your child might like to colour in the pictures they have drawn.

Place a sticker here.

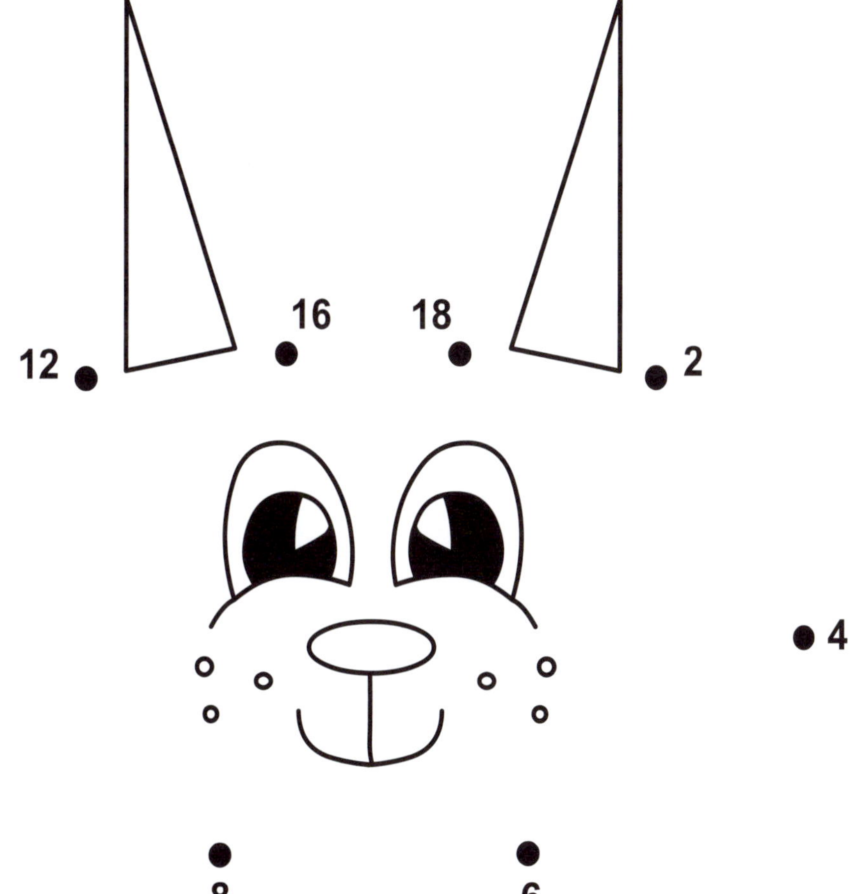

2. Help your child draw your own dot-to-dot picture counting in 2s.

Place a sticker here.

Counting by 10s

Some things might come in 10s, like apples in a box, or spots on a leopard. There are 10 apples in 1 box, and 20 apples in 2 boxes. Write the numbers that tell you how many things there are altogether.

How many apples?

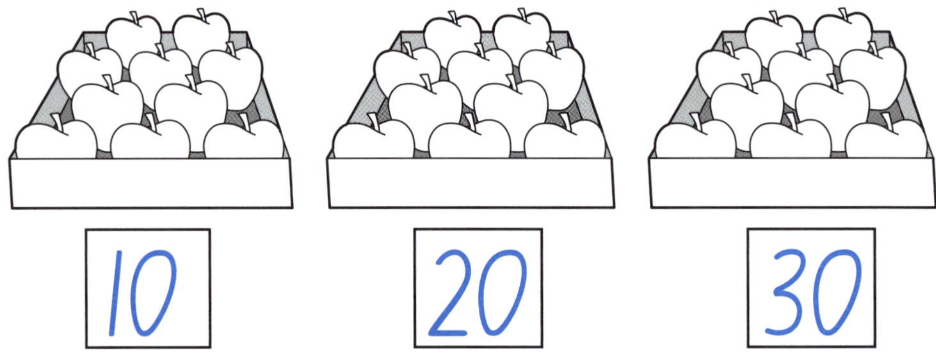

How many legs?

How many beads?

1. Help your child practise counting up by 10s, eg. 10, 20, 30, 40, then up to 100.

Place a sticker here.

How many marbles?

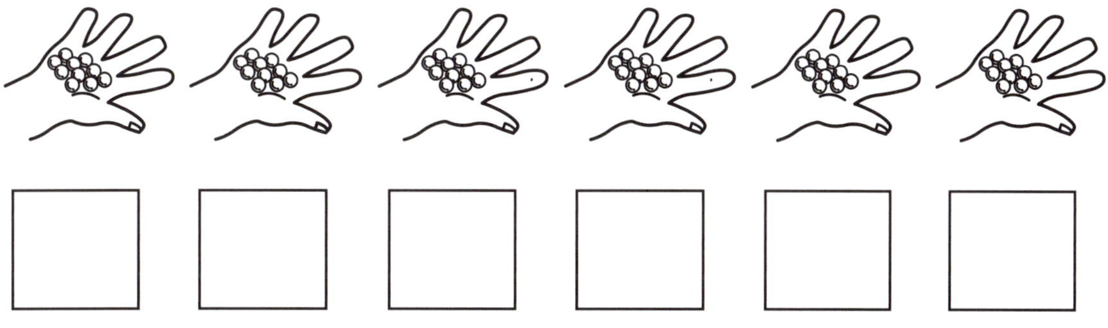

How many beans?

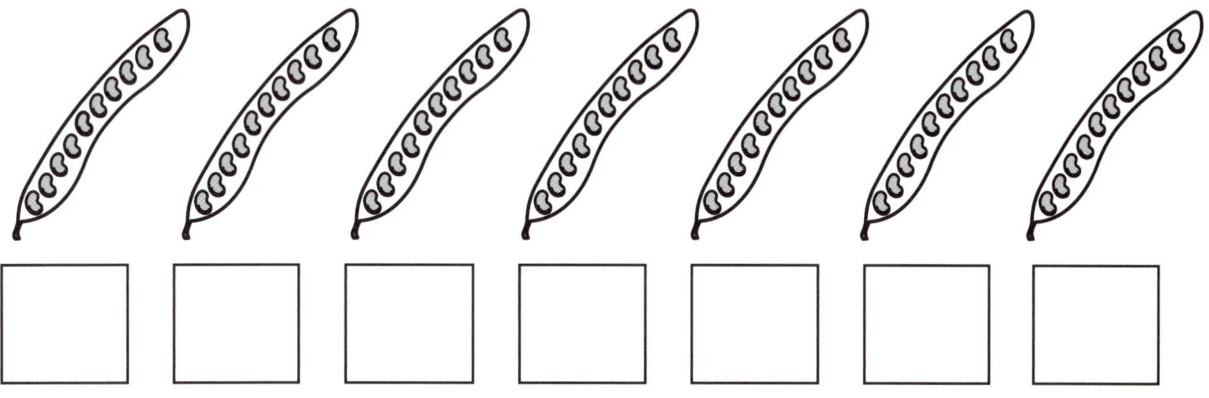

How many spots?

2. Ask your child to flash 10 fingers as they count up by 10s. How far can they count?

Place a sticker here.

Drawing groups of 10

Draw the missing pictures in each group. Then count in groups of 10 to find how many there are altogether, eg. 10, 20, 30. Write this number in the box.

Draw 10 petals on each flower.

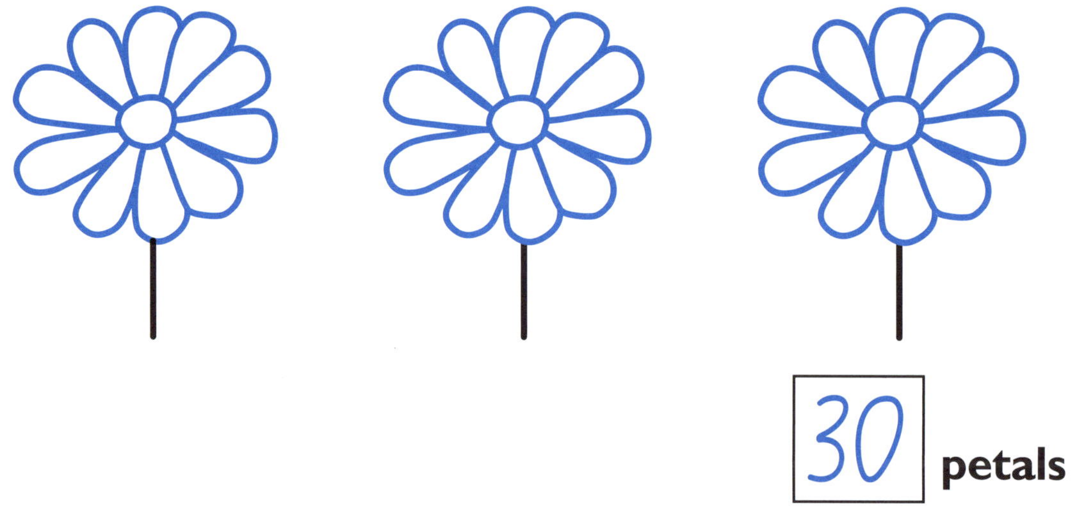

30 petals

Draw 10 apples on each tree.

apples

1. Throw a dice and draw a matching number of faces on a sheet of paper. Then ask your child to draw 10 hairs on each one.

Place a sticker here.

Draw 10 stripes on each caterpillar.

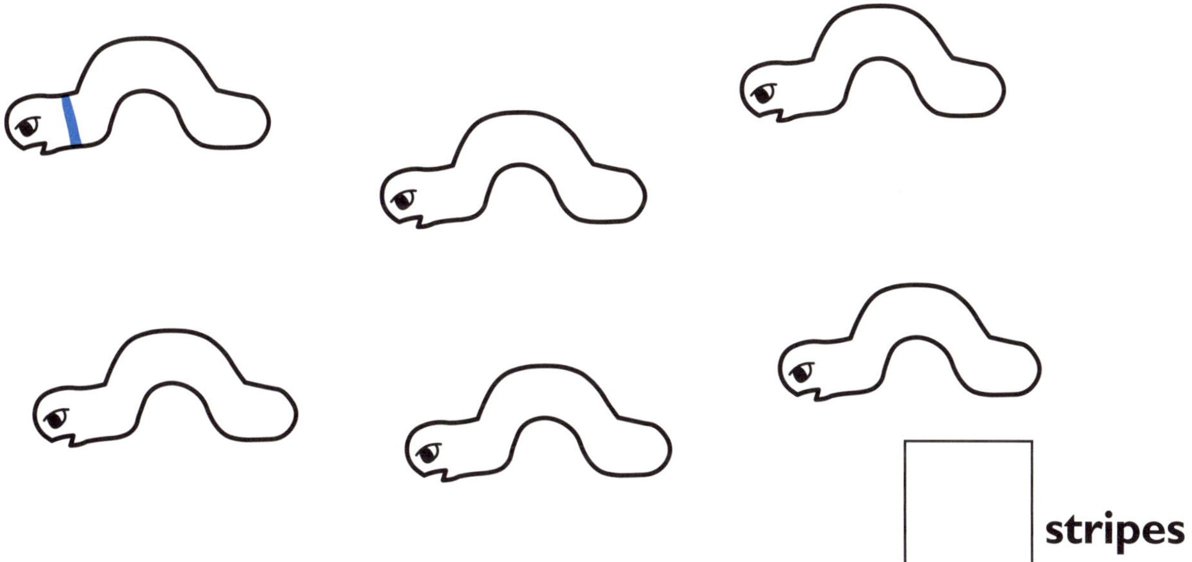

Draw 10 spikes on each cactus.

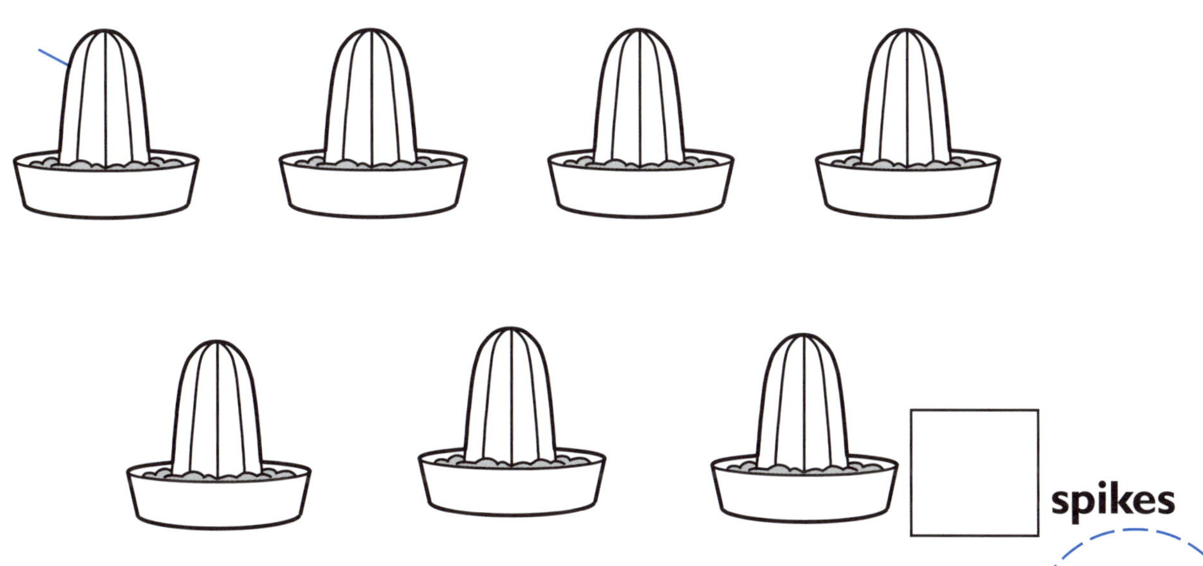

2. Ask your child to jump up and down 10 times. Can they jump up and down for 6 groups of 10? How many jumps is that altogether?

Place a sticker here.

Drawing more groups of 10

Follow the instructions to draw groups of 10 circles or triangles. Then count by 10s to find how many there are altogether. Write this number in the circle at the bottom of the page.

Draw 5 groups of 10 squares.

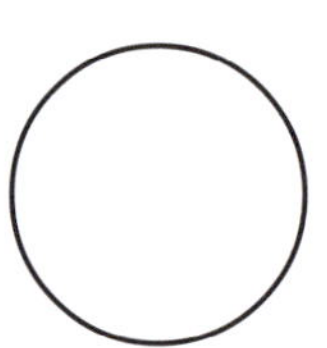

squares

1. Throw a dice and draw a matching number of faces on a sheet of paper. Then ask your child to draw 10 freckles on each one.

Place a sticker here.

Draw 7 groups of 10 triangles.

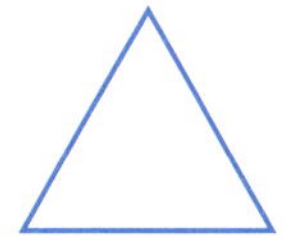

2. Make up a simple song or rhyme counting in 10s to 100 to help your child remember the sequence.

Place a sticker here.

Finding groups of 10

Count how many animals are in each group. Write this number at the top. Then draw a line around each group of 10 creatures. How many groups have you made? Write this number in the square at the bottom.

How many bees? ☐

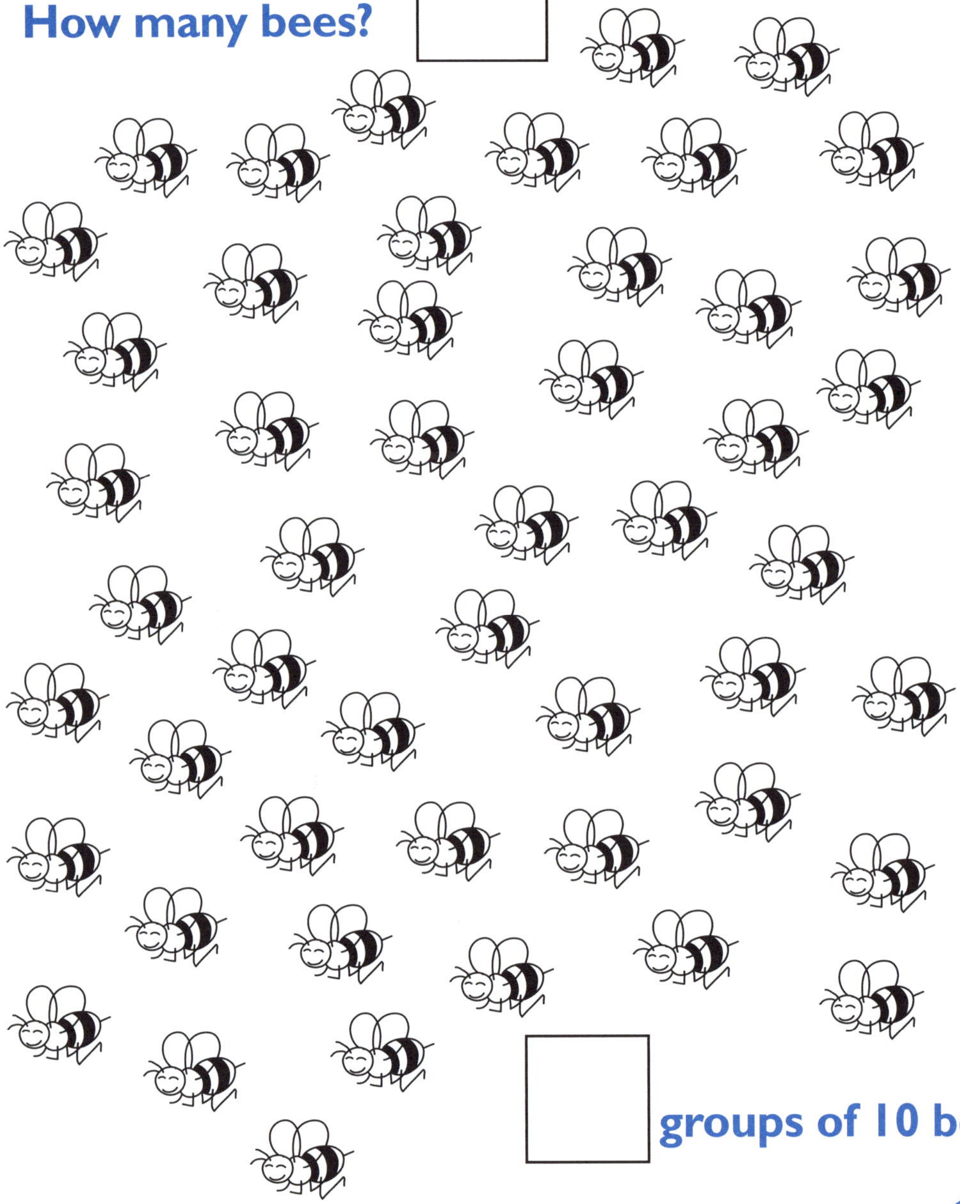

☐ groups of 10 bees

1. Tip out a jar of buttons or other small objects. How many groups of 10 can your child make?

Place a sticker here.

How many ladybugs?

groups of 10 ladybugs

2. Scoop up a handful of leaves outside. Ask your child to arrange them into groups of 10.

Place a sticker here.

Making a fair share of 10s

Sharing objects is easy! To share 60 peanuts between 6 monkeys, draw 1 peanut next to each monkey, counting up as you go. Then add another peanut to each monkey, and keep doing this until you reach 60. How many peanuts does each monkey have? Write this number in the box. Then do the same with freckles on the next page.

Share 60 peanuts equally between 6 monkeys.

How many peanuts each?

1. Take 30 straws and ask your child to share them between 3 glasses. How many straws in each glass?

Place a sticker here.

Share 80 freckles equally between 8 faces.

How many freckles each?

2. Ask your child to share 40 coins between 4 purses. How many coins in each?

Place a sticker here.

Joining the dots by 10s

Here are 2 hidden pictures. What do you think they might be? Start at 0. Count up by 10s and join the numbers in a line to make the pictures.

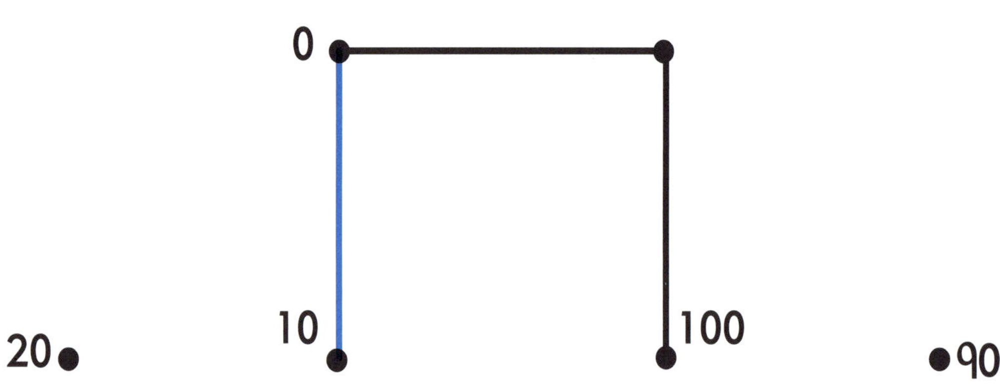

30 40 70 80

50 60

1. Your child might like to colour in the pictures they have drawn.

Place a sticker here.

10 ● ●90

0 100

30 70

20● ●80

40 ● ● 60

50

2. Ask your child to try counting backwards from 100 to 0 by counting in 10s.

Place a sticker here.

Counting by 5s

Some things come in 5s, like fingers on a hand, or toes on a foot. There are 5 fingers on 1 hand, and 10 fingers on 2 hands. Write the numbers that tell you how many things there are altogether.

How many fingers?

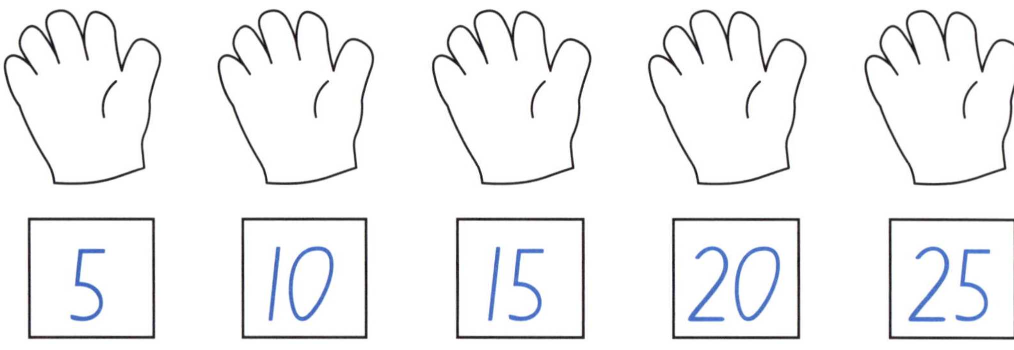

How many crayons?

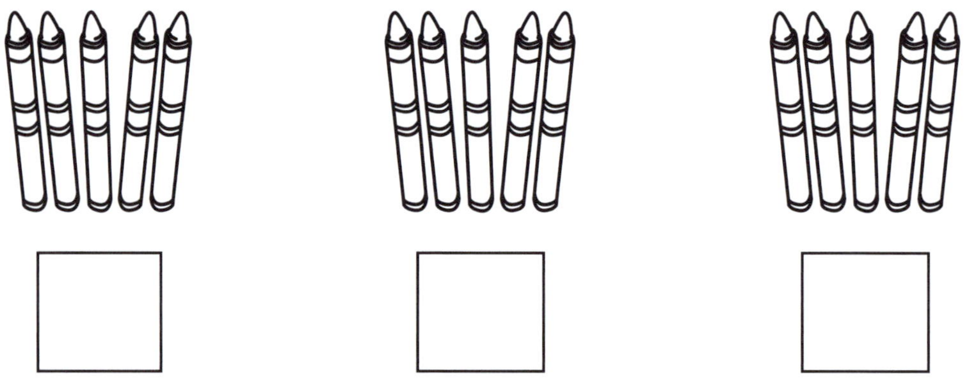

How many beads?

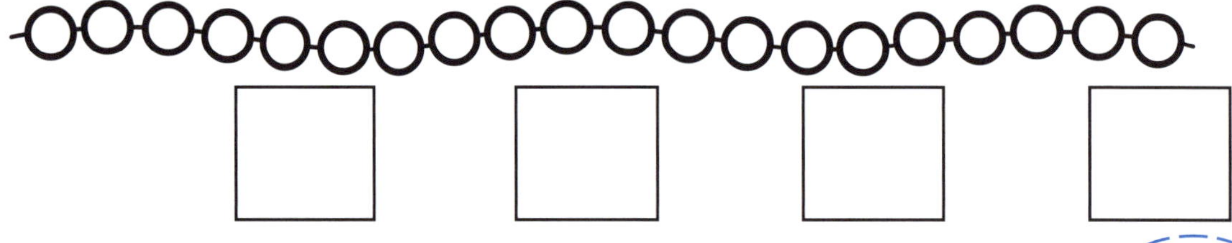

1. What else comes in 5s? Have a look around you for other objects that you can count in 5s.

Place a sticker here.

How many dots?

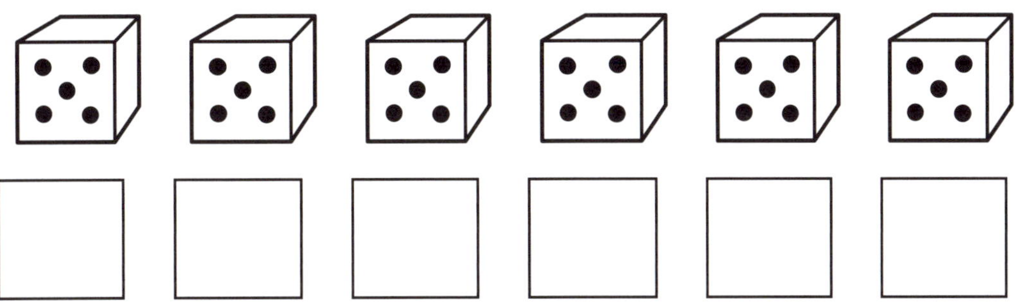

How many hairs?

How many bananas?

2. Ask your child to flash 5 fingers as they count up by 5s. How far can they count?

Place a sticker here.

Drawing groups of 5

Draw the missing pictures in each group. Then count in groups of 5 to find how many there are altogether, eg. 5, 10, 15, 20. Write this number in the circle.

Draw 5 stripes on each zebra.

20 **stripes**

Draw 5 eggs for each hen.

eggs

1. Throw a dice and draw a matching number of frying pans on a sheet of paper. Then ask your child to draw 5 sausages in each pan. How many sausages altogether?

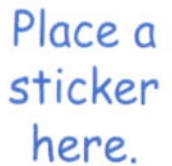

Place a sticker here.

Draw 5 beads on each string.

beads

Draw 5 peas on each plate.

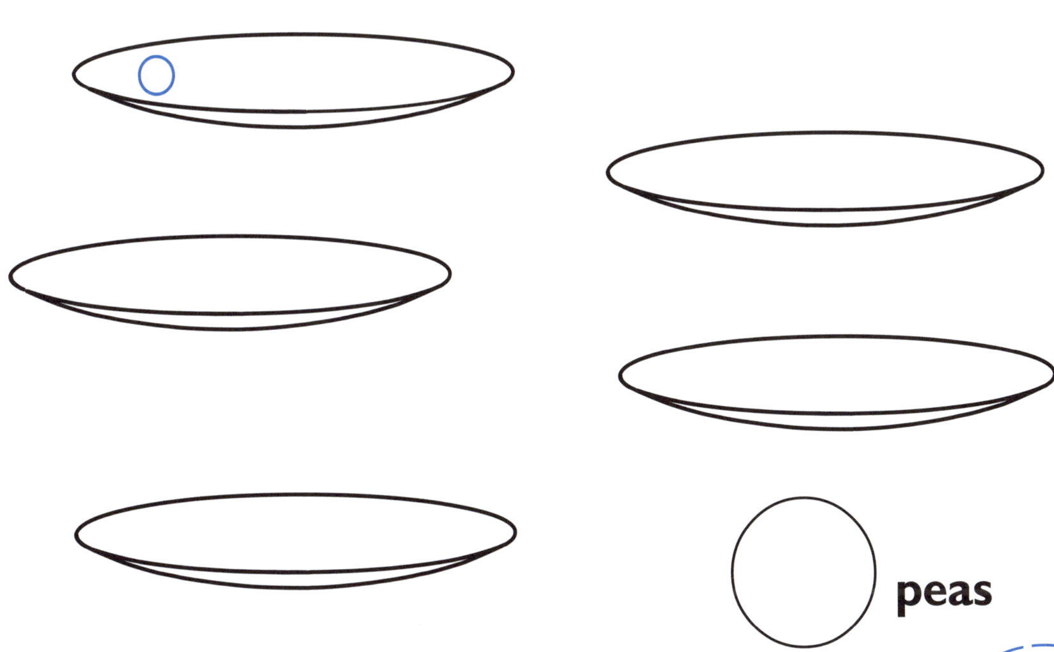

peas

2. Ask your child to clap their hands 5 times. Can they clap their hands for 6 groups of 5? How many claps is that altogether?

Place a sticker here.

Drawing more groups of 5

Follow the instructions to draw groups of 5 shapes. Then count in groups of 5 to find how many there are altogether. Write this number in the circle.

Draw 2 groups of 5 squares.

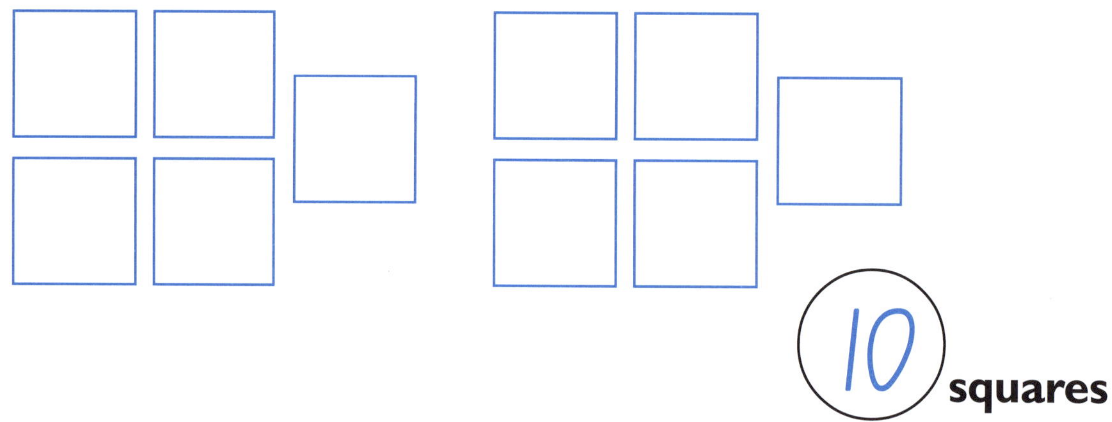

Draw 3 groups of 5 triangles.

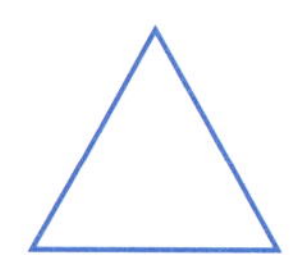

triangles

1. Help your child say each 'number story' out loud. For example, '2 groups of 5 squares makes 10 squares'.

Draw 8 groups of 5 circles.

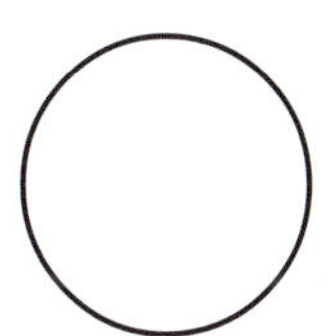

circles

2. Ask your child to lay out 4 groups of 5 cards. How many cards altogether?

Place a sticker here.

Finding groups of 5

Count how many animals are in each group. Write this number at the top. Then draw a line around each group of 5 animals. How many groups have you made? Write this number in the square at the bottom.

How many koalas?

groups of 5 koalas

1. You can try this activity with real objects, such as small blocks or bottle tops. Ask your child to divide the objects into groups of 5, then count them by 5s, eg. 5, 10, 15, 20 and so on.

Place a sticker here.

How many kangaroos?

groups of 5 kangaroos

2. Ask your child to close their eyes and see how far they can count by 5s.

Place a sticker here.

Making a fair share of 5s

Sharing objects is easy! To share 35 candles between 7 cakes, draw 1 candle on each cake, counting as you go. Then put another candle on each cake, and keep doing this until you reach 35. How many candles does each cake have? Write this number in the box. Then do this for the biscuits on the next page.

Share 35 candles equally between 7 cakes.

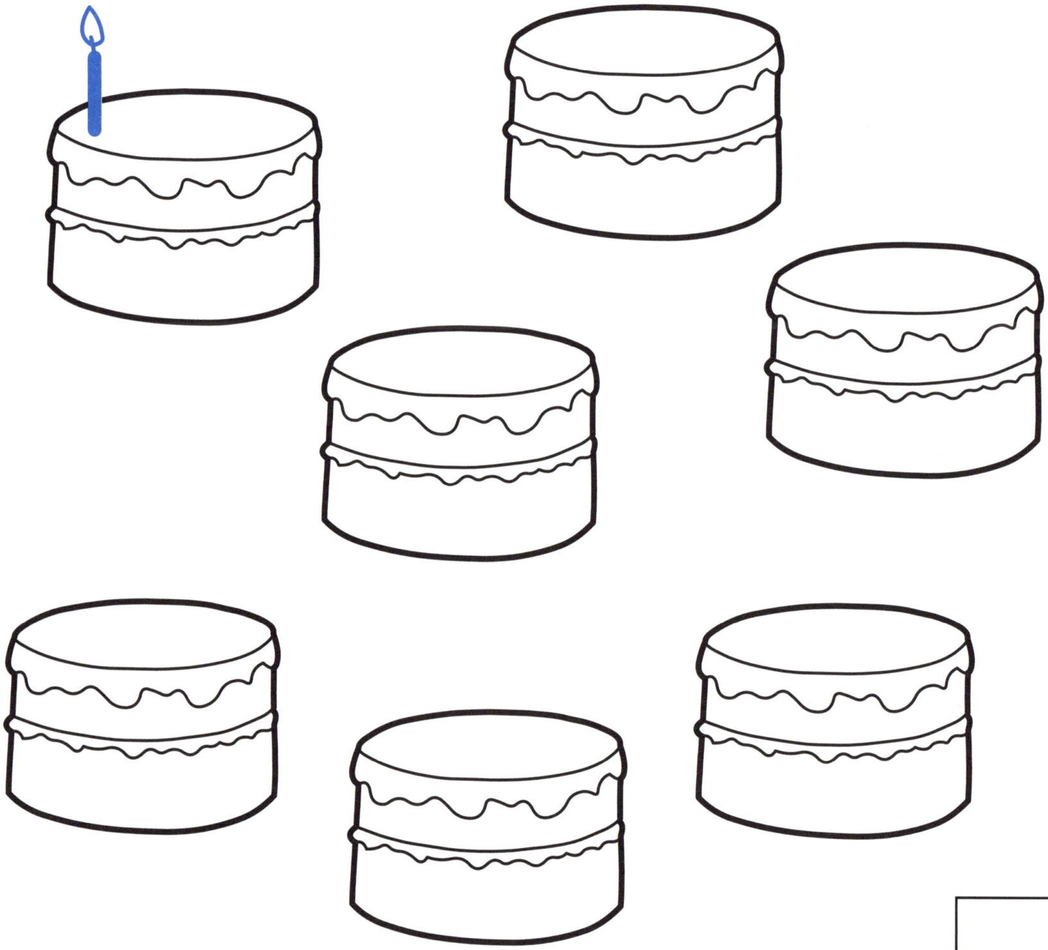

How many candles each? ☐

1. Collect 20 buttons and ask your child to share them equally between 4 people. How many buttons does each person get?

Place a sticker here.

Share 50 biscuits equally between 10 jars.

How many biscuits each?

2. Ask your child to share 30 pencils among 6 people. (You can draw the people on a large sheet of paper.) How many pencils will each person have?

Place a sticker here.

Joining the dots by 5s

Here are 4 hidden pictures. What do you think they might be? Start at 0. Count up by 5s and join the numbers in a line to make the pictures.

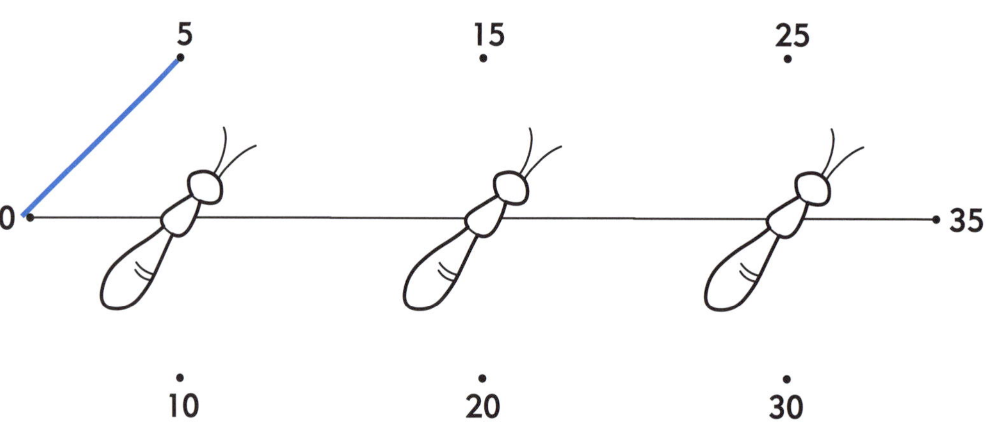

1. Your child might like to colour in the pictures they have drawn.

Place a sticker here.

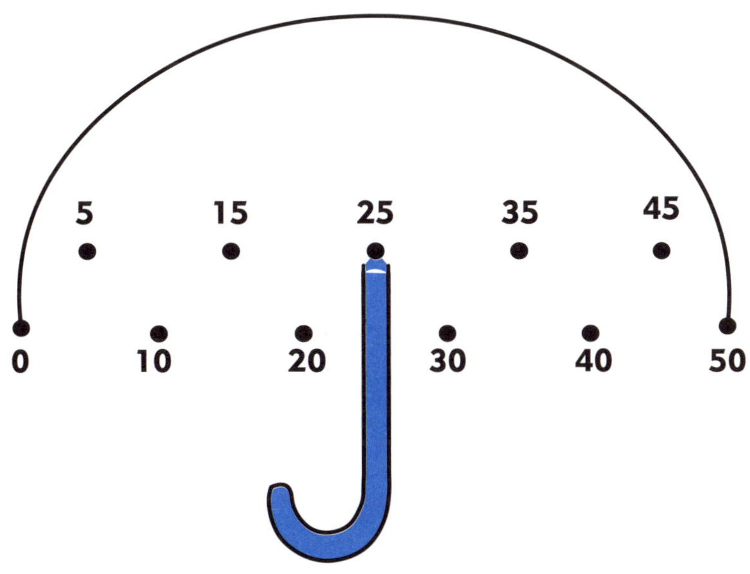

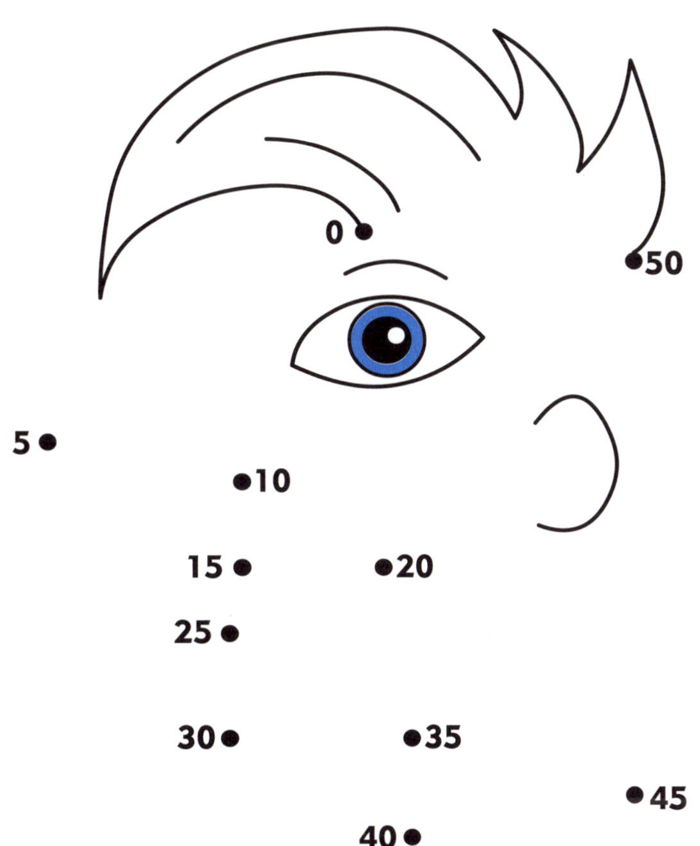

2. Count up by 5s with your child, then ask them what number comes after 10 when you count in 5s. Which one comes after 20? After 30? Can they see any pattern?

Place a sticker here.

Counting by 2s, 5s or 10s

How many objects are in each group? Count up the objects and write your totals in the boxes underneath as you go.

How many fingers?

10 20 30

How many caterpillars?

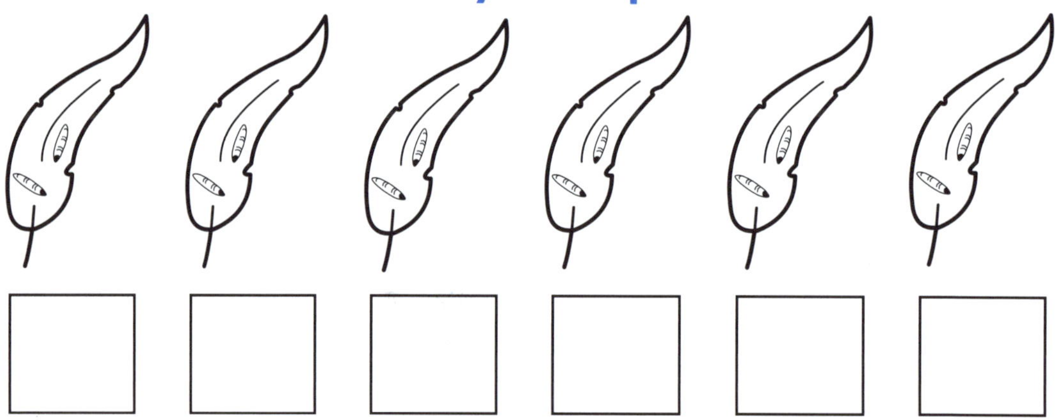

How many legs?

1. Ask your child to touch each picture as they count aloud by 2s, 5s or 10s.

Place a sticker here.

How many petals?

How many candles?

How many dots?

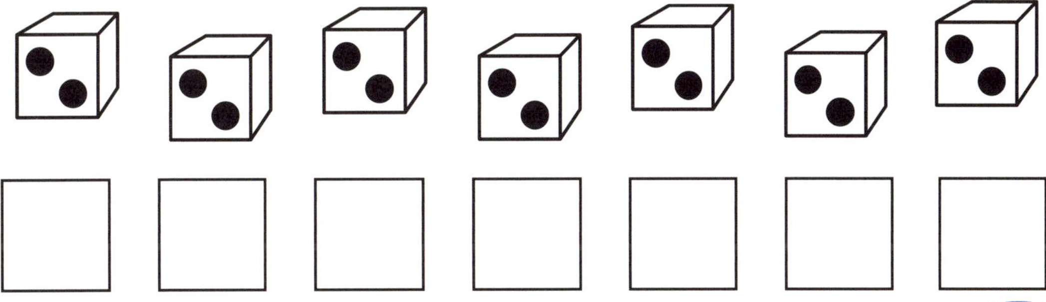

2. Ask your child which is their favourite way to count: in 2s, 5s or 10s? Why?

Place a sticker here.

Drawing groups of 2, 5 or 10

Draw the missing pictures in each group. Then count in groups to find how many there are altogether, eg. 5, 10, 15. Write this number in the box.

Draw 5 frogs on each lilypad.

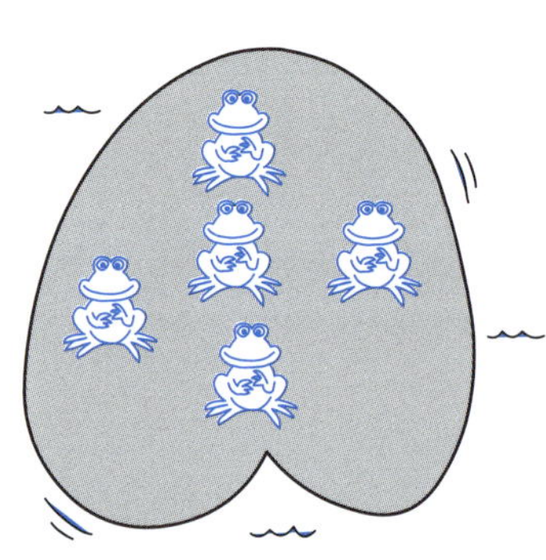

Draw 2 eggs for each hen.

eggs

1. Make a set of number cards for counting by 2s. Turn over one at random and ask your child to count up in 2s starting from that number.

Place a sticker here.

Draw 5 olives on each pizza.

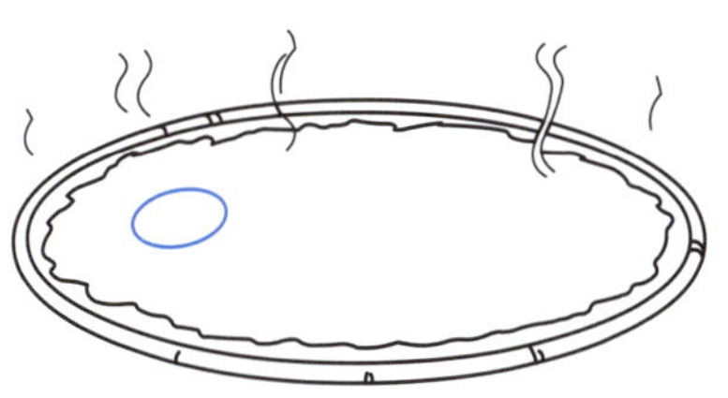

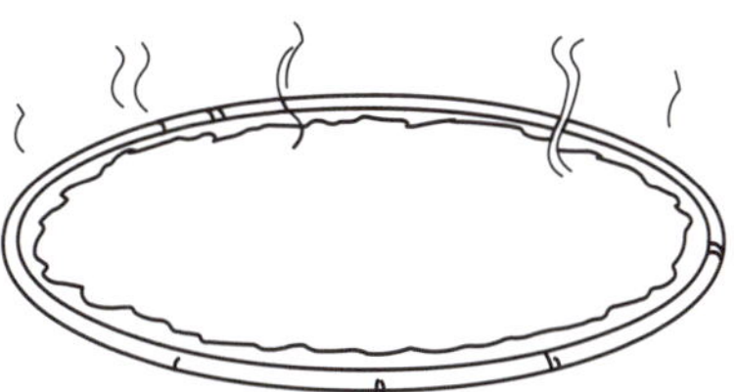

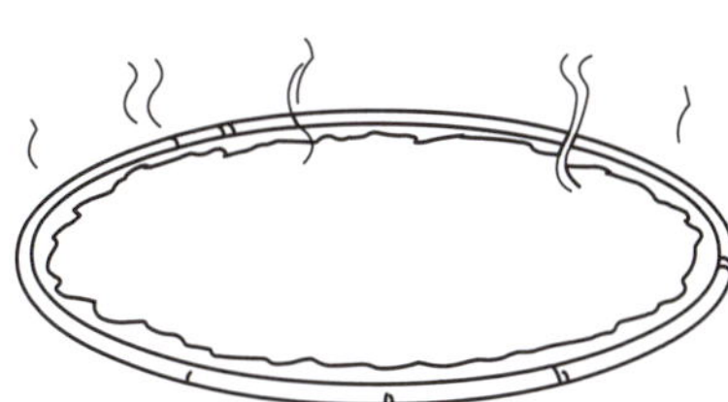

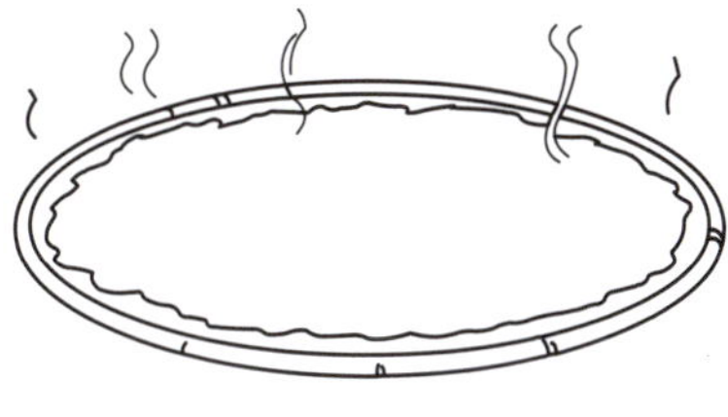

Draw 10 spots on each leopard.

spots

2. Ask your child what would happen if you had one more pizza to put 5 olives on. How many olives would there be now?

Place a sticker here.

Finding groups of 2, 5 or 10

Count how many animals are in each group. Write this number in the top square. Then draw a line around groups of animals as asked. How many groups have you made? Write this number in the square at the bottom.

How many giraffes? ☐

☐ groups of 2 giraffes

How many monkeys? ☐

☐ groups of 10 monkeys

1. Give your child a group of counters, then ask your child to group them into 2s, 5s or 10s.

Place a sticker here.

How many crocodiles?

groups of 5 crocodiles

2. Put all the hands of your family or a group of friends together and ask your child to count up the number of fingers in groups of 5.

Place a sticker here.

Making a fair share

Sharing objects is easy! To share 18 caterpillars between 9 leaves, draw **1** caterpillar on each leaf, counting as you go. Then put another caterpillar on each leaf, and keep doing this until you reach 18. How many caterpillars are on each leaf? Write this number in the box. Then do this for the apples on the next page.

Share 18 caterpillars equally between 9 leaves.

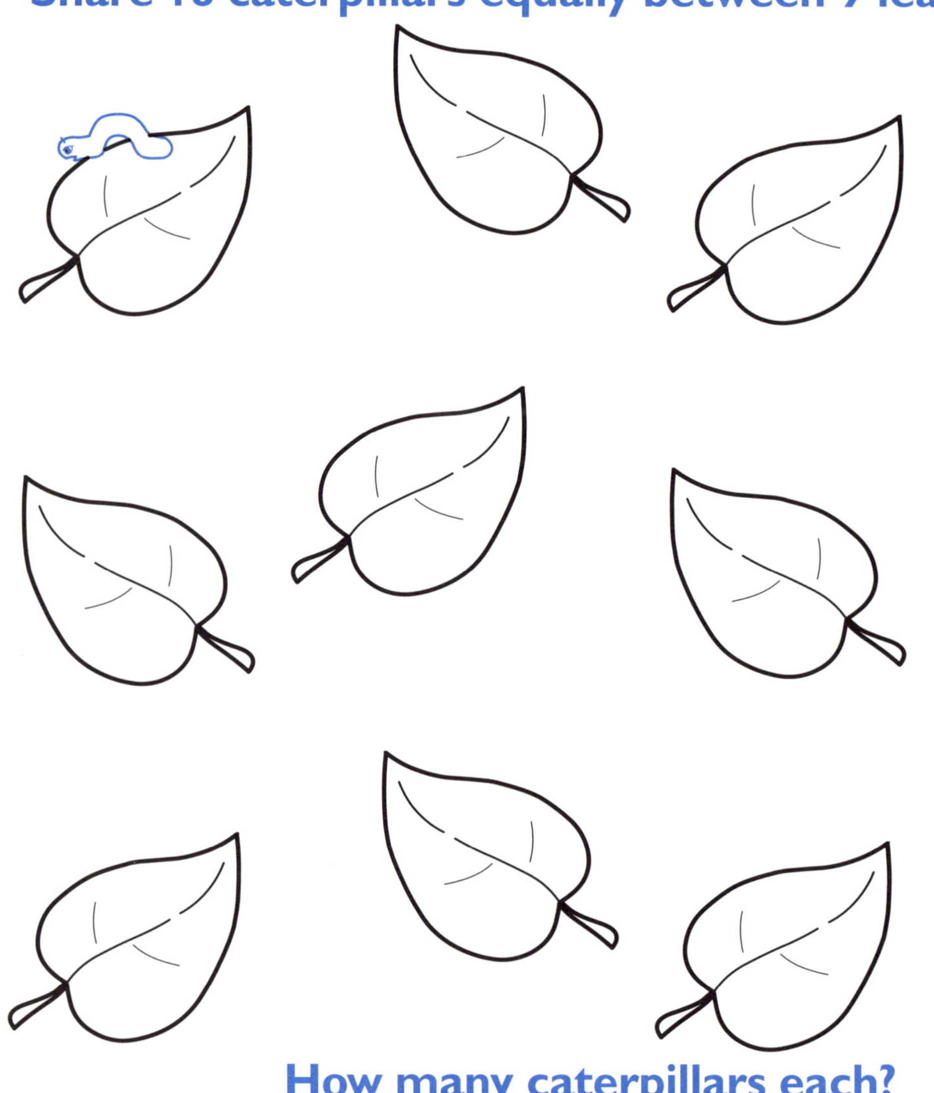

How many caterpillars each?

1. Make twenty $1 coins out of cardboard, and ask your child to share $20 among 4 people. How much does each person have?

Place a sticker here.

Share 30 apples equally between 6 trees.

How many apples each? ☐

2. Next time you set the table, ask your child to help you share utensils equally among the places at the table. How many utensils does each person have?

Place a sticker here.

Writing the missing numbers

Fill in the missing numbers on each snake, counting up by 2, 5 or 10.

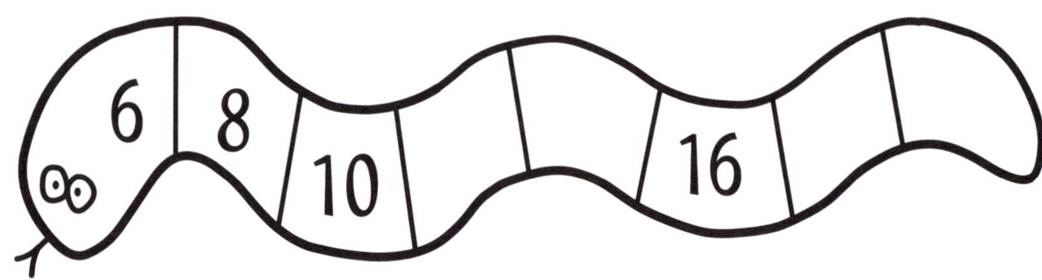

1. Help your child practise counting aloud in 2s, 5s and 10s. Can they count up in 2s starting from 10?

Place a sticker here.

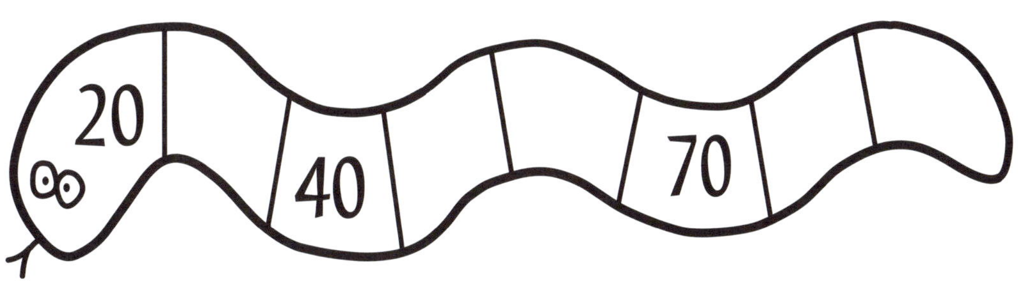

2. Can your child count up in 10s starting at 30?

Place a sticker here.

Well done!

You have finished the book!

Place your last two stickers on the picture. You can colour in the picture, too.